A Lack of Good Sons

A Lack of Good Sons

Jake Arthur

TE HERENGA WAKA
UNIVERSITY PRESS

Te Herenga Waka University Press
Victoria University of Wellington
PO Box 600 Wellington
teherengawakapress.co.nz

A catalogue record is available at the National Library
of New Zealand.

ISBN 9781776920112

Published with the support of a grant from

ARTS COUNCIL OF NEW ZEALAND TOI AOTEAROA

Printed by Blue Star, Wellington

For Todd, sine qua non

Contents

A pack of dogs.
A sneak of weasels.
A lack of good sons.

Jim Nevis

It was after *Holmes* had started,
so it would have been gone seven,
past my bedtime.

I stood on the window frame,
toes hooked like a monkey's,
hands on the glass, looking through
the tropical Northland downpour
for something to witness.
That night, I found it.

Bored of the bush, I turned my head,
pushed my other cheek to the cool glass.
My eyes floated over the gravel road,
dilapidated barns, cotton buds of sheep.
Then I saw it. I didn't understand
what it was. Then I sort of did.

Jim, the farmer, Jim Nevis, stood on the grass,
naked in his black gumboots,
just there in front of his house.
His pale body was shocking,
like the inside of an oyster.

He was facing away from me.
I could see his sagging bottom,
his hairy back. He turned around.
I wanted to hide but I was frozen.
My stomach felt like it did
when I walked to the bathroom
in the black country night.

His chest hair ran down like seaweed,
the type that stank up the beach.
I stared and stared. Was my heart
knocking too loudly on the glass?
Were my parents seeing this?
His penis was a pale fish bone.

This alone was mystery enough
to get on with, but, when he walked back
to his house and climbed onto his deck,
he kicked off his gumboots.
And I realised
he hadn't really been naked before.

I got down from the window
because I felt so strange.
I thought I knew it all,
but here was a book just legible enough
for me to realise how little I could read.

I agonised for a week
about whether to tell.
I said the word 'naked' to myself
under my duvet, louder and louder
until I was so scared by my own daring,
I held a hand over my mouth.

Mum wheedled it out of me in the truck.
She threw her head back and laughed.
'Honey,' she said, stroking my hair, 'oh, honey.'
She thought for a moment and said:
'You used to do that when you were little, too.'
She smiled and started the engine.
That was it.

I sat silent, thinking.

I knew this was different. Jim Nevis wasn't little.
What he'd done had *meant* something.

Hockey

Criss-crossed spotlights pop on
making a bright green dome
under the world's fading blue one.

The triplicated shadows
show potential plays:
to backtrack, strike out, cut across.

Sticks arc the astroturf, hit mighty *clacks*,
one girl pulls her mouthguard
along a shining line of spit, and yells.

The sounds and the lights,
the choreographed violence
hair and sticks swooping together . . .

My scalp tingles and I drift over the court
thinking about the difference
between soft and hard woods.

Afterwards, I wait for Rachel's
face to tell me the result.
She kisses me, lips cold with sweat.

I drive her home dazed
by the yellow streetlights,
her hand hot in my jean pocket.

Duelo a garrotazos

I killed my father
in a meadow turned to mud
by our brawl and blood.

His herding cudgel met my temple
in a spray of pain as a cloud
gave way to blinding sun.

I looked down at my shirt
and saw red candlewax
that wouldn't out in the wash.

He stood sweating, thick-set,
greying and remorseless,
huge as a hill, as dumb and heavy.

I felt pleasantly hot from the blood
and the day, as fast as he was slow,
as good and right as he was bad and wrong.

He lunged. I stepped aside
with mild, drunken grace.
Then I drew my own cudgel back and

swung it down with such wild force
that when it hit my body was exhausted
of every energy and sagged

beside, half on top of
my dead dear dad,
like a tramp over his last sack of potatoes.

Damage limitation

Like when you make
a joke no one laughs at
and decide to shut up.

Like when you are caught
in a lie but come wonderfully
admirably clean.

Or like when you accidentally
kill your neighbour's son
backing up your car
on the way somewhere
you could've walked to
and from then on you live meticulously
not rustling your bag of Maltesers at the movies,
guilty for days after a woman tells you
to put your dog on its lead
at the playground.

And of course, it goes without saying
that you can never drive again,
though you loved it, the feel
of it, it reminded you of your
mother who would get into a fight
with Johnny or Sam or Brian
and take you for a long, winding ride,
'Down here, you think?' she'd say, or,
'Let's just see what's round this corner'—
it's one of your earliest memories,
her hands moving around the wheel,
no strain on her face, just calm, lunar attention
and when you got your driver's licence—

well, if only you hadn't
you broke a life, broke lives,
and now that's over
being easy with everyday things
you've reached your quota of damage
and this so early on.

Milk

I have never felt such milk
in my life
it is a variety of milk
that was unthinkable to me
people recognise my milk
from the news
I cry of milk
in the night in the morning
in the afternoon of milk
everything before
(and there was milk,
my life has by no means been milkless)
was a poor imitation
of real drop-everything milk.

Doze

My dad knows so many women.
Nights at his are female.
I hear their voices in the wall,
their comings, their goings.

In my half-sleep I dream of
a hand hitting a tambourine,
its ringing reply like a laugh.

The fan thrums over me,
drying my sweat cold.
The bedsheets twist me awake just
as I feel I'm falling—

A second's dazed panic
as the door slams.
The key in the lock.
The night and him talking.
My leg hanging off the bed.
The streetlights on my fingernails.
Is coming nothing? is going?

Space

Christmas Eve

A planet compassed in rings
spinning in a confusion of stars
like a mariner's golden astrolabe.

I hang up the washing, turn on the fans.
The drops hang and slowly move off,
a hesitant rain. Outside, the planet.

The waterless mop leaves streaks.
I rub them away with a towel.
It takes a whole sore day.

Outside, the planet. Inside, I think about
'generations'. How many since . . . 1900? 1500?
Chains of people, water seeping into earth.

Or a sneeze, contagious.
Achoo: a generation—spraying out, thousands.
Bless you. *Gesundheit.*

The planet shrinks, a gold medal, a gold coin.
I hope it is not crying out for company,
for who will visit it next, and when?

Christmas Day

A huge rod of iron and ice
so big it's just texture, glistening grey,
though tip-toed I can see the end of it.

I call it God's bridge. We drift beside it.
It looks made; huge hands sculpting in the deep,
a potter's wheel at the centre of the universe.

Why not? There are plenty kilns for firing,
clay for shaping, giant marbles in a thousand colours.
One like blown glass with a leaf in the middle.

God's bridge has pools on it: carbon dioxide.
Silver shivers, like mercury. What joy
to splash through puddles in gumboots.

I sat on the beanbag in the viewing room today.
I should ward against this idleness, was taught to.
But that was so long ago.

In the middle of the night, I ran a marathon.
The stars came no closer. The bridge loomed
the same all 42km. But the windows misted up completely.

New Year's Eve

My new book is about King James I.
He hated smoking and wrote a book saying so.
It was called *A Counterblaste to Tobacco*.

Lothsome to the eye, hateful to the nose . . .
nearest resembling the horrible Stigian smoke
of the pit that is bottomless.

So, I woke up today wanting to smell,
thinking about surströmming and sea-salt,
about coriander and the durian I couldn't eat in Singapore.

I thought about that gold planet, from before,
and tried to draw it with the felt-tips
we are given in the 'Recreation Box'.

The gulf between my imagining of it and
what I can put on the page makes me sit back, annoyed.
I have drawn a child's sun. Only the smile is missing.

Outside, the bridge is moving away.
I imagine standing on the edge, beaten by solar winds.
Below me, Styx. The smell of its water.

Twelfth Night

I thought about death all my free hours today.
There is nothing outside but the wallpaper of stars
which no longer holds any pleasure for me.

Epiphany

Out here, you can turn and turn in bed
and wait for the dawn forever,
your back getting sorer and sorer.

Tonight (and this time it *is* night, 2am) I traced
all the decisions that led me here back to my ex,
the one who would squeeze my breasts like dog toys.

He said I was a dreamer who'd never get anywhere.
And here I am, nowhere. But the stars, the solitude:
nowhere as destination.

I visit my frozen work-family in their pea-pods,
and watch over them for an hour, love hungry.
Then I do a Depression Inventory.

1 point: It takes an extra effort to start doing something
2 points: I have to push myself very hard to do anything
3 points: I can't do any work at all.

I scrape a pass, and go back to bed.

Confessional

In the cathedral,
our conversation honeycombs.
He is not so different as I hoped.
Some of what he says
I wear heavily.

Passing through the ancillary chapels,
he shows himself through
the lattice of the confessional.
This is just one of my things, he says.

My bowels were moved for him.
His hands were myrrh on the lock.
He seemed like the answer to a question.
He drove all the branches into the trunk,
back along the roots.

You are altogether lovely,
but there is a spot in you.

On a pew I rest my head and look up,
the colonnade a forest to a stone ceiling;
in me, too, an awful lot of rock.

Peregrination

I cavorted through the Gobi Desert
I fell in love with a camel in Saudi
I poured pints in Kraków.

If anecdotes are a life, I have lived.
Otherwise, I've urgently wasted my time.

Perhaps I'd better have stayed
quids in at my old gaff in Perranporth
walking my childhood cliffs
holding the arm of my late nan
looking for the sea in the mist.

But what stories would I tell her?

Bare choirs

The mast when it creaks
is reminded of itself
when it had branches,
a wealth of leaves, anchors
in the ground.

It sounds off, by being alone.
Its voice used to have a choir
to add to when it bent to,
each trunk a pipe in
a fathomless organ: a deep collective
murmuration and the treble of the wind
through the canopy.

But, here it is, sawn and shorn,
grafted to these unnaturally arranged
woods from far-flung places,
dry to its core amid all this water.

The way it moans the ship's rightward yaw,
The way it echoes when struck,
The way it falls silent.
It knows that it's alone.

The flap and licking
thrump of the sail is a beat,
the slapping waves an uneven melody,
but it is more dirge than music
and not a tune to sing to.

So says Chiron

There's going to be a moment when you say:
must I always be interdicted?
That's the moment you walk out the door.

Oh, but Achilles, with those fingers!
Play me the lyre again.
Doors will open *for* you.

You haven't four legs, but you're quick.
Quick to learn, slow to laugh,
heavy to carry, light to wake up to.

Mothers—forget them! Mine was a mare.
And think not of the world;
you'll be yoked to it soon enough.

Enjoy the time that's passing.
The season's mixing hues . . .
Today's redder, don't you think?

Disbelieve omens. There's something in them,
the problem is *what*. I see men
carrying you, killing you, kissing you.

There's going to be a moment when
you remember how we used to play,
and it'll feel as remote from you as the spheres.

Best stay here with me.

Big weather

Her face, where storms
passed, where clouds cast
shadows over rainy eyes,
he made his diligent study.

Like a grandson rancher
in familiar country, he forecast
morning from eve, rarely mistook
the clues in the dawn's aspect.

To live with the weather
not despite it, to be steady—
this was the life's work
he didn't know he was doing.

Like a good animal he followed
the secret mandates of his nature,
and was rewarded with kisses,
surprise harvests, seasons of joy.

He was a craftsman
who couldn't name his craft,
but she knew it was work
to stand straight in the wind.

To find rough seas
reason to stand firmer still.

Soft lips

Soft lips like mine used to get
playing the French horn two hours a night.
      Soft lips a pink overflow
      in the Tubby Custard Machine.
Soft lips
      in the faces of the girls I date in my dreams
      and whom kiss after passionless kiss disappoints.
Soft lips, on you, on me,
      on the man on the TV and his son and *his* son after that,
      and every patronymic Softlips issuing thenceforth,
            pursed before opening to reveal
            another creased sheet waiting to be thrown over a bed.

The forecast

No creatures left
to cup to the window,
or to sluice plugwards.
The bees are dead
in their stalls.

This topside grave we sow
with silk for flowers,
our last good glass
toasted to payday credit!

Oh, help.

I look at the road
that wends down the mountain
and think of the insects
spatchcocked on my windscreen.

All these thundering machineries
to wax so fat and wane so thin
and give up the ghost all the same.

Young waverer

My brother's shaved legs coming out
of the flat surface of the bathwater.
He tells me I can touch them, but I don't.
I sit beside the sink and he points
his toes up like a ballerina and sighs.
Remember this day, he says. And I do.

Do you know what sex is? Yeah, I say quickly.
Well, he says, I've had it, and it's amazing.
I only hear my heartbeat—What's it like?
It's like . . . a promise you make with your body.

My brother receives a love letter, blue-inked and long,
he kisses each page and gets me to do the same, for luck.
I know this means he's leaving so I do what he says.

If we do it, will you promise not to forget me?
Ew, that's not how it works, idiot.

Tuesday and he's gone. Mum asks where.
It was me, I cry, and drop hot tears on my pillow.
I find the love letter under his mattress and try to read it.
My hands are shaky and my stomach is sick.
The words are covered by bright red kisses.

Fish

The spook and the crater lake.
The fish in the wine goblet.
A shadow on the house.

Putting the book over your nose
so that you are of it, breathing
in a very small space until the air
is hot and wet and doesn't fill you.

I am sick of being clever in the dark.
I am sick of feeding the fish, the fish-
feeding, the Sisyphean fish-feeding.

The giant goldfish in my dream
was the colour of a ripening peach.
It put me in its mouth.
It had such a saintly countenance.

When I poured myself into the glass,
I floated upside down, not a body but
a lack of one, or of light, altogether.

Hair

Let me tell you about my hair.
It followed behind me like a mousy river.

Left to drag, its train picked static from the carpet.
It raked the leaves when I checked the letterbox.

My follicles had a condition: 'extra hard
workers that don't know when to quit'.

The dog lay on it, my brothers spat Hubba Bubba on it.
Dad despaired when I sat combing at the dinner table.

Yes, I was the school pariah and ate my lunch with the weeping willow,
but I never felt a victim to my body.

Mum told me the tale of a male Rapunzel
every princess dreamt of finding, his keratin rope that wanted climbing.

Mum said that one day a girl would part my hair
and wrap it around the both of us.

The Great He-Goat

No one else wants the chair.
The witches throw themselves on the ground,
grunting, legs and skirts splaying.
A fat woman picks between her toes.
Nobody looks at me, so I stare freely.

The racket their blathering makes!
But are they saying anything? Their language
is all bubbles and hiccups, up and down;
they talk over each other, never listening.

Yes, *that's* it: they never stop moving;
they are preternaturally restless. Their fingers
cannot be still and so seem to tremble. Always
they wring them, rub them together, click them.

Like walking into a crypt, a damp chill rises, wind stills.
The women fall quiet and pull shawls and hoods
over their carbuncular faces and jutting noses.
I put my hands in my muff and sit.

Something is coming; the witches look around.
Cracking noises in the woods all around us.
A sudden yellow glow. Panicked whispers.
I steel myself. What part is this?

Then He is there, the He-Goat.
His metalled hooves bore into the soil.
He carries a child wrapped in a sheet.
His black robe drags across the dirt.
The hum of the women sounds of locusts.

A voice, as if in my head,
human words on an inhuman tongue:
Welcome our visitor.

The witches fall silent.
Their slumped bodies come taut, backs lengthening boards,
their hands go still, their noses seem to recede.
Under their hoods I see not muddy straw but fine ringlets.
They turn, one body with many gorgeous heads, to look at me.

Hark

A tattoo covers the birthmark on a man's arm,
branches of a tree, eyes in the trunk.

I understand why choosing
a mark might feel better
than being assigned one,
though I couldn't do it.
I would look at a million designs
and die having chosen nothing,
my arm as empurpled as the day I was born,
when the nurses mistook it for blood
and wiped at it, in vain,
again and again.

Lads

Spare the china, these are boys:
heavy, febrile bodies that crack
into, open, up, down.
Between their legs a glock,
their arms guns.

These are boys:
who fight drunk outside clubs
or in car parks or in cinemas over eye contact;
who win fat lips and black eyes,
and stories to tell to other boys.

These are boys,
but think of parents: their line of sight,
their outsized sons padding the hallways,
jarheads with a six-pack punch,
weaponising their bodies five times a week.

Think of parents:
cleaning the bore of the barrel
checking for fouling of the rod
taking apart his action
finding him faultless.

Lot's wife

A woman can be as shrewd as the sorghum farmer
saving for his ugly daughter's dowry.

A woman can always balance the cheque book,
and still, in the end, be frustrated.

There are forces at work
to obstruct wifely planning.
These are husbands, fathers, sons,
and, if the former subvert them, daughters.
I am ever waylaid by men's tempers.

Though some say He may be She,
you can see His sex in His means.

Think of the great tower stretching to the sky,
and the dauntless city we now mourn. Think of
the saplings in my window I thought sure-fire,
but that, like the rest, fell to ashes.

Think of me, the loveliest woman my age,
all resolved—come apart in particles—falling through
your fingers to spring up again unyielding as rock.

And this for a slight!
A final glance at the life I knew, the home I loved.
For this, he unworked me.

Wane

My heavy son, penned in his chamber,
carried away, divided, broken
into daily tasks of mourning.
There is grief in a desert, grief in a jungle.
There is a parched ocean named after me.

When will I receive my woman's body?
I am all girl. There is a dry channel through me
that no amount of money can bring to flow.
Beside the banks I wait, clutching sand.

Mercury, ascendant (and he to his core dry),
shone over death, as in my birth, and told me
to *pull myself together*
but like the torn handles of a plastic bag
I fell to strips, too late and little to swaddle him.

I am inundated with nothing.
I have never broken my banks.
I once put myself into stirrups just to imagine;
I yelled; I went red in the face. I even wore the gown.
I screamed for a day and bore nothing.

Fatal familial insomnia

'The rare genetic disease ███████████
█████ capable of undergoing ████████████████████
a change in shape ██████████████████████
██
the prions begin to create ███████████████████
████████████████████████ abnormal prions
███████████ percent of brain cells dead.
Abnormal prions ██████████████████████
████████████ and attack the thalamus, seat
of sight and sleep ████████ are 'distracted',
the host is fitful ███████████████████████
██████████████████████████████████████ cannot rest
may lose their memory ████████████████████████
███████████████ reported to speak in tongues.'

The daughter of the woman
who died of the killer prions
was sure she'd inherited them.

She wore a veil at the funeral,
thinking of her mother's red eyes.
She lay on her childhood bed,
imagining her mother's pacing.
She couldn't sleep and wondered
if it was the disease already.

After a week, though, she did sleep.
She returned home to her own life,
though it didn't feel hers, wholly, now;
she read the tea leaves with her friends,
walked the dog and went to bed early,
fatigued in every sense.

From the doorway
her boyfriend watched her sleep,
her chest rising and falling.
He pictured the cells in her body,
wondered what shape they were
and what they were capable of.

Call time

For the longest time
my morning coffee passed, black,
through my lips and ran, back, down my gullet.
It darkened my chyme and
was never heard from again.

Until this August.
Like birds dropping out of the sky
a local newspaper could have run with it,
my freak occurrence. Instead
I ran with it to the bathroom.

That bad month gave me time to think
and slowly I realised: it's the coffee.
Once, coffee was fine. Now, it wasn't.

One epiphany sprang into the next
like a fire in a fire factory.
—Of course!
This is what Obama meant by Forward
after he'd finished with Hope.

My organism had called time on coffee
as it would call time on all things.
There'd come a day when not only would I
not know the difference between chyme and time
but not know *between* and *difference*,
and, until then, I had to drink tea.

Hand-eye coordination

The ballpark figure she wants
is the silhouette with a sloped back.
His body is a long, curved articulation
of her lifelong privations. He springs, dunks.
She wants him sometime in the next now.

Hairy legs out the shorts and the socks
halfway down (designed to excite her?)
the risible *school*-ness of his uniform
its attempt to hide what for years has been
a sexual machine, awaiting work.

Tanned shoulders, a muscled arm, a glimpsed armpit,
the full disclosure of his nylon shorts (!).

She is a brimming sink of desire
but—just like that—the plug is pulled,
and the boy over the road is safe again.

Shamir kibbutz, 1974

The bees hid the sound.
I was aware only where on the ground
I stepped, wanting no stray drones to collect.

I clicked a tray in place as a bang went off
—stood, listening, to the warm apiary air.
Another, then, that sounded like a cough.
I was so green, a foundling, a stumbling deer.
Something's fallen over, I thought, offhand.
A sweet mistake from another frontier:
you never hear a gunshot in Auckland.

I walked out to hot summer,
June in Galilee, and to four men with guns.
Strange, but my mind went first to the number.
Four, hippies wearing bandanas, four men.
There were only *two* men assigned to bees.
Plus the guns, that was something else again.
I realised by the slowest degrees.

And then I saw everything was yielded
my friends and fiancé, my family,
none of whose warnings I thought I needed.

When it was too late I took in the scene:
the great grey dolmen in the sun's spotlight,
a sepia horse at hay, the daytime moon,
bees flying to nectar in the Golan Heights.
And me, checking out of the commune.

You and the view

Palm trees are only festive
until you see them from the passenger seat
on the way to a funeral
or after a long, difficult conversation,
in which nothing gets resolved.

You wore all your faces wrong today,
especially that smile which is almost never Right.
It appears at the oddest moments.
I want to say—
but I have been warned off saying.

Among the mosaics and trickling water,
I ask myself if I am a boring person.
Sometimes I think I may never again
have an interesting thing to say.
This is an obstacle to you loving me.

Later, when the heat is suffocating,
you sit in your boxers by the balcony,
the film set of palm trees behind you.
I sit all the way over here on the bed.
There must always be a perfect thing to say.

I daydream about a change of scenery.

Encounter

Now that we're all talking about aliens
I can tell you about my abduction
though I don't like that word
it was more like a visit
I was made to go on
and it happened
at eight in the morning
when I was in my garden
planting out for the spring
I got pins and needles in my neck
which is not all that unusual at my age
but then my brain came out in gooseflesh
and my arms got longer and longer in front of me
now *that's* odd, I thought, because I could reach the hedge
I could grab the powerlines and touch all the roof tiles—
next thing I knew I wasn't in my garden anymore
but sitting inside what looked like a letterbox
someone had got me a jerry can of water
and a single cracker on a dinnerplate
it was something that my grandson,
who's five, would serve for supper
I wasn't alone, there were two
shiny tubes, red at the top
like metal cigarettes
—these were the aliens—
for some reason I wasn't
even the least bit surprised
I knew I had to do my best to represent
and I did quite well, answering their questions
about juice, trigonometry, gender, and flags of the world
for good measure I asked them a few questions of my own
about how long they'd been doing this, whether they enjoyed it

they seemed to like the conversation a lot because their tops got redder
in the end they had the decency to drop me home, though upside down
but that was sorted soon enough and I'm used to getting soil out
of my clothes, being green-fingered, but first I looked up
in the hope of spotting their craft and
I did see a little black shape but
probably it was just a bird
oh well, I thought,
from a distance
everything's
unidentified.

The stones

Beware by me,
the earthy fumbling
of the body's organs—
hammer stirrup anvil—
a sperm whale
sleeping vertically
like a bullet in the deep.

Beware of the mind,
what can it not say?
That a landmine is lonely,
that it feels the rain
in the clotted dirt
awaiting a mate,
fulfilment and release?

Beware by me,
an easy lay to toss
off a lectern
and get lost among
the sweaty paper
of others' work,
or forever misplaced
as if by an architect's
slip of the pencil.

Beware of the mind,
that it reasons unreasonably,
that the stream may run empty
and flow with rocks and stones.

Spear

I want to float out of my mind and into my body.
The body is better.

With a body, I could draw him in
for a kiss.
With a mind, I could only stop
myself doing that.

Talking to you in the observatory while you cried.
Sometimes I can take
a long time
to feel.
Like a boomerang you forgot you threw, etc.

Don't worry!
My inhibitions—my mind—they run into my very balls.
I may not be very principled (after all), and that's a thought,
but you are a form that shapes, a regular pattern,
a whole that encloses and a network that connects
and I can't just walk,
formless,
away.

The Fates

(1) Atropos

'The age of heroes is over,'
announced the woman with the scissors.
The strings were tough to cut that day:
she thought of a cow's thick hind,
the corded muscles of slain men.
Her scissors were small and plain,
tijeras you could pick up at any euro-store,
but they cut in a hundred dimensions at once,
severing all the fibres that tether souls.
With each cut, she saw death's bloody variety.
Violence. Accident. *Flagrante delicto.*
These men were not used to losing;
some of them spat her name as she sliced away.
She didn't like this, but kept it to herself.
Only the work mattered, and, as it was endless,
she had to get on with it.

(2) Clotho

'The age of men is begun,'
said another woman, plucking at the distaff.
With her right eye, she watched her spindle;
with her left, she saw each birth, bloody and alike.
She began to pull the threads out so quickly
that her fingers themselves seemed to spin.

The pace of the women increased.
They worked so fast they did not notice time.
Their hands worked but their limbs contorted.

(3) Lachesis

'The age of men will end,'
exclaimed the third woman, surprised;
her rod found the new-spun threads all the same length.
But what different lives! They unfurled in her eye.

Suddenly, it was over.
Atropos's scissors cut the last strings.
Finding no more, she looked over her shoulder at
Lachesis, who, fiddling idly with her measuring rod,
turned to Clotho, whose distaff was a bare stick.
They stared at each other.

Bluejackets

The unlucky mariners, huddled in the cave
shoulder to shoulder, backs against the salt and the sea,
trying to stick their breath in their lungs
that their bodies might stop shuddering.

At the very back where the stone comes down
like a curtain, the old captain sits cross-legged
over a candle. His is the only still body there
because he has just died, water leaking from his nostrils
in two threads, as though he were a full jug of brine.

No one has noticed he has died except the hermit
whose poor shelter it is to share, and to him the threads
look like stalagmites, grown up from the rocks over years
to reach the captain's body where, perhaps, they will
bloom and branch in the still-warm innards of his brain.

Grizzly, adj.

Where was the bear
when he was named *grizzly*?
Not at a seat around the table.
Not with a marker at the whiteboard.

Collins, Webster and Merriam, Sir Oxford,
they were there, wouldn't miss the chance
to swivel chairs and biscuits in their saucers.

The bear, he was elsewhere,
at home in Saskatchewan
watching the salmon in the river,
silver leaves of a flooded bush
waving with the water—
hungry, yes, and pensive
in the luxury of knowing where
his next meal is coming from
but in not eating it just yet.

The bear will use his paws to crush the fish
pink, raw and brineless, and carry them
into his hot muzzle, which, it's true,
has white hairs in it—is grizzled—but he's not
in a grizzle, far from it, life is bearable, is beary.

Springer Motors, 1976

At the lot,
he watches a young couple
stupid with love hanging
off each other's arms,
eyes catching, invisible hooks.
The man's wearing a suit because
he thinks that's what you wear
when you buy a car and she's all
dolled up, but her hair not too tall,
her eyes not too smoky, cos that's how
she thinks you look when you buy a car.

This couple is his replacement,
their love a keener, newer version of his.
Harry sees them as an omen of his death.
There is a line of people waiting to replace us,
he realises, newer model, more cylinders, better machines:
they'll last longer, work harder, fuck better, be happier.
He's already being phased out.

He pushes back his hair,
wipes sweat off his forehead.
100 degrees outside and the air-con can't cope,
just hums and costs him a buck in power bills,
but you've gotta have it, Toyota makes sure of that,
all a part of selling people on the brand, or something,
as though people weren't buying a car at all but
a sensation, crinkling rice paper or a trickling stream.

And there's probably something there, the Japanese
know what they're doing, know more than we do,
America's getting lazy, too many fat cats,

a diet of milk and honey will do that to you.
The way they work, you see them on the news
bashing panels together, crossing streets
with their identical suits and briefcases, going
someplace, going to overtake us in the 80s they say,
but what can you do? Everything dies.

He tries on a smile, tightens his tie,
and goes out to greet the young couple.

1588

Everything was animated.
It spun on a dime. It was umami.

Now I know better.
There is a sameness in everything.

There is a terrible
sameness to everything,
is anyone else aware?

I have ejaculated maybe
three thousand times.

The ships, the Spanish ships!
They are in the harbour, they
have left buoys in our hearts.

Intercession

In the un-light afforded by the eaves
my son tries to change into his togs without
getting naked in front of his friends.

His furtive squirming—I want to lay wisdom
like so many petals around him.

Only confidence stops the laughing

In the way of confidence is only fear

But fear takes years

But how, to have his ear without pulling it?
To be firm when so obviously in love?

Out of the shadow he looks up, sees me,
and, ashamed, stomps off to the pool.

Eclose

I'm so tired of caterpillars.
This is a difficult stance to maintain
when you are an entomologist.

But if I have to hear one more lecture
about *heterocampa obliqua* . . .
What about those creatures who cannot
just curl up and change the way they are?

I used to kiss dolls together, like every girl did.
I, too, used my bed as an altar to speak to God.
But I can't be the only one hypnotised
by their father tying his tie in the hall mirror.

People ask me why
I have devoted my life to this ugly class of beings,
just big enough to be disgusting.

The answer was a fascination with flight,
the logistics of two pairs of wings, as graceful
on six legs as I was clumsy on two; it was
the fact of bodies built to camouflage.

These hold little pleasure for me now.

It's taken me a long time
to get, I suppose, where every girl has gotten,
and I am not quite there, yet.

But I am more attached to the human
than I have ever been, and less disposed to hide.

Saturn devouring his son

I was so hungry I ate my son.

So you see,
it's not so complicated.
Nothing *psychological*
about it.

My eyes look like that
because he was terribly,
terribly chewy, as are all
the ungenerous animals,
of which sons, I grant you,
rank worst.

Asmodea

The bull charges at the red sky
that in shafts through the bush
maddens him. Afar, muskets crack.

His horns pick up branches and
cobwebs and clawing *enredaderas.*
He strains, useless;
his great head is stuck fast.
Afar, a woman screams.

Near, a crashing in the bush:
the bull's eyes turn plates in their sockets
to find this new threat.

A small hard thing hits his flank.
The bull snorts, his tail flicks and
hooves scratch at the dry ground.

The boy who is the small hard thing
feels what he has hit before he sees it.
This is a bull. This is a dangerous creature.

But he sees it's caught, its horns snared,
and the danger is nothing to what he's left.

He runs his hand along the bull's side,
sees it huff out hot wet air, and whispers:
Tranquilito, señor toro, le ayudaré.

As the boy works at unravelling the knots,
the bull lowers its snout between his
arms as if they were the rim of a water-trough.

It reminds him of the priests at prayer,
so meek in their kneeling that their foreheads
touch the cold stone tiles of the church.
The bull seems to deliver its life up to him.

And it is like he is back, tying sheaves of grain.
It is like the French never reached them at all,
which is what everyone had promised him.

The boy frees the last vine from the bull's head.
Before the horns swing, they gleam red in the sunset.
The next second and he is gored to death.

Sine qua non

Two flecked sons of proud stock
dressed as soldiers, lying on the dunes,
saying their *without which, nothing*s,
their words so low and their khaki
matched to the sand's terraces so that they
are almost invisible, almost indivisible,
their dark hair and beards yellowed in the dust
so they look American (one says).
The other laughs, making his dry lips dark with spit.
Because it is hot, unusually hot and still—
which is why they are having this quiet, serious talk—
his friend's laughs are like a cooling breeze.
He turns onto his side and tells him to turn too,
so that one man blows sharp, relieving air at the face and neck
while the other talks quietly and seriously
about fears of losing more people.

He in the harp

I watch him play his sad instrument.
It feels wrong to play a harp in a garage.
It leans into his shoulder like a drunk friend;
his fingers hold it up, right it.

He works by negation. Not this string, not this;
his hands run a schoolyard pick. Not him, nor him;
and hovering—until finally—*him*.

His fingernails go white under strain.
I feel like I am staring at his soul,
or that he is holding himself open
and I am darting the in-between.

Heart strings, sure, but deeper,
the Old Testament word for heart, which is bowel.
To be in his heart. To pluck his love.
So he works his sad instrument.

The dawn with us in it

Sod in the gutters coming off
in black snakes I throw down
to the garden, shreds of tyre
that disappoint the roving dog.

I creak back on the corrugated sheets,
examine the cut on my hand.
The threat of tetanus, more or less
likely than falling off the roof?

Seeing death up here, I think of you
who are sound and kind,
restless and meticulous.
Terrified of dying.

We are mixing like
this dirt and these leaves,
these waters and weeds
to make some tertiary thing.

I climb down the ladder
wishing myself dissolved into parts
to be shot through with your better ones.
Something like the waters
now sluicing clean the drains.

Lung

My brother was having a lung removed.
'Just like Pope Francis,' the nurse said,
'and look how long he's lived!'

After the surgery, he would wake up
thinking he was suffocating. From my bed,
I watched his back heaving in the dark
and thought of a leaking paper bag.

There were complications; he became devout.
After that, the crucifix hung around his neck
alongside the cords of his nebulizer.

I took up swimming. I held my breath underwater.
I came second in the school cross-country.
I would sigh loudly around him,
expelling litre after litre.

Once I held a pillow over his head, as a joke.
'Don't be a drama queen,' I said, when his eyes bulged.
Then he passed out.

Lying by the pool in the sun,
me in my togs, him in his jeans,
he reached over and put a hand on my chest—the right side.
I shivered, though he wasn't cold.
My chest rose and fell.
He took his hand away.

King of collisions

Snow falls in spring streets in Paris.
Two *policiers* side by side on horses.
Their hooves kick the white powder along . . .
Suddenly I am Nikolai racing back over the ice
from a night at Uncle's, cousin Sonya on my lips.

Natasha! Dead Petya! Petruschka!
They live encased in a snow globe
Napoleon put a crack in. A few flakes
fell out, only to land in twenty nineteen,
and they chose right here to do it.

I am not ready. I am not ready.
I say to them, I stand, and I say . . . *privyet.*
What a nutter they think I am! The policemen
think I'm another *touriste* who speaks no French.
They just nod, the gesture of wide berth.
Oh, oh, and the flakes are dissolving.

Imagine Petya as a grown man, head free
of bullets. Try to imagine Natasha as anything
but an old babushka (you can't!). Imagine
Maria, striking flint at the altar and in her heart.

But here are the policemen. If I don't move we will
collide—France and Russia—collisions
are the pricks of light we read history by,
but at some point it is bright enough.
(Petya died bathed in morning light.)

But, and I say this to the officers, but
we won't remember anyway. Eventually

no one will be losing sleep over it.
God, at the end, when he is weak
and tired and covered in snow, will say:
I can't remember what happened
but I *do* remember the people.

So says Ophelia

You tumbled me.
Like a vase on rocks,
I went everywhere.

Then was I called
a document in madness
a page in a strange book
you were writing for me.

A grimoire of girls!
The spotting on my knickers,
ink from the devil's pen;
the lack of it on the night,
by Cock, I am to blame.

Young men will do it—
courtiers, scholars, soldiers
they'll eye, tongue, and sword
but young ladies mustn't,
must be patient and weep a-time
and get hitched, by God, get hitched.

Envy pretty peasants, maids,
those low, free girls who roam
and—sure—cry by rivers, but
what joy it must be to sob a chest-shaking sob!
My tears are silent, shrunken violets,
another vetoed seeping, while I sing on,
hey non nony, nony, hey nony.

But now I am out, about!
Ready fellows tough luck—

but this slug-a-bed's heard verses enough.
I'll sing in the court, if I so wish
I'll be-herb my hair, if I so wish
I'll live in the willow tree, if I so wish.
Good night, ladies. Sweet ladies, good night.

Sasquatch

Tonight, at my dinner date,
I kept thinking about the sasquatch,
and in particular: what is it? where is it now?

It's not that my date was hirsute.
I could tell from his chin
that he had less hair on his legs than I do in winter
so perhaps it was the hairs clinging
to the mussels in their tomato marinade
or the fact that the first peach had
fallen from the tree in the courtyard.

But, as far as the sasquatch, I would throw
hunks of steak onto my begonias if I knew I would
be keeping a legend alive in the process,
and my garden is a patch of my soul.
Finally, I would have an act of faith!

Conversation eluded us like
the mussels did my fork
and I wanted to shrug and say:
We have different-coloured tongues.
But there was a pot plant in my peripheries
that when I squinted, as I do when bored,
looked like the hair of my best friend from kindergarten
and I chorused to myself:
Jenny McDonald!—she had
gone into a coma and woken up with a
longing to paint chrysalises—it was almost
something one could make
a conversation out of.

But nothing passed between us, not even the bread.

If you imagine the sasquatch always on the run,
you reach a point of empathy, but he
was just sitting there with his mouth closed
and I found myself hoping he would foot the bill,
or be swept up the Empire State in a silk dress
that would make the most of his pearl-bare legs.

Changed opinion as to flowers

Here, reader, an oddity:
a daisy chain left on the squat rack,
a fragile thing with stitched limbs,
on the safety hook—and the weights
a solid 200—he who left it here lifts.

What do daisies say? Given like
a child's necklace between careful thumbs,
imagine he carried it, hung it and replaced it,
and there it lies, gleaming and slowly dying
under the fluorescents.

A chain is connection, a daisy speaks play,
but this gift is a message he could not read.
So he left it here, hooped it over the peg
as though decorating a neck, leaving
with a changed opinion as to flowers.

Tracy Island

Your square glasses
I didn't get to know
except on Instagram,
but they suit you.
Make you look like
a Thunderbird. Was
your favourite T3?
Or was it the yellow
one, coming out the
belly of the green one
like an *Alien* payload?
Let's Airbnb
Tracy Island, I'll
lift my drawbridge
if you blow my palm
trees down, but only
if after we can talk about
the hidden things,
like the launch pad under
the swimming pool,
and what I really think
when I see you
in your square glasses.

Fleet

I receive a love letter.

So begins a sunshine interlude.
I am ringed with fronds
I am evolving vestigial organs:
webbed feet, a tail, a pouch
made only for dreaming.

I am seeing in kaleidoscope,
and I am in love with it!
I am seconds away from everything.
I am the bullseye of the world.
Goodbye forever!

Acknowledgements

Some of these poems have been published in other places. 'Sine qua non' and 'Lot's wife' were published in *Sport* 45. 'Changed opinion as to flowers' was published in *Turbine* 2015. 'He in the harp' was published in *Mimicry* 1. 'Confessional' was published in *Food Court*. 'Spear' was published in *Sweet Mammalian* 3 and 'Sasquatch' in *Sweet Mammalian* 1. I would like to thank the editors for their diligent work and excellent catches, and the many early readers of these poems for their comments and their forbearance.